Dr. Steve Vandegriff

Foundations of Youth Ministry

Editor: Joann Manos
Cover Designer: Doris Bruey

Foundations of Youth Ministry

Copyright © 2006 by Steve Vandegriff, Ph.D.

All rights reserved. No part of this publication may be reproduced or transmitted in any form or by any means, electronic or mechanical, including photocopying, recording, or any information storage and retrieval system, without the written permission of the publisher.

Requests for permission to make copies of any part of the work should be mailed to:

Permissions Department
Academx Publishing Services, Inc.
P.O. Box 56527
Virginia Beach, VA 23456

Printed in the United States of America

ISBN-13: 978-1-60036-021-3
ISBN-10: 1-60036-021-1

Foundations of Youth Ministry

FOUNDATIONS OF YOUTH MINISTRY

Striving for Maturity

I. Teenagers are beginning to _____.

    A. Instead of asking "_____?" they're asking "_____?"
    B. They are learning to define their _____, _____, and _____.
    C. They begin to use humor, especially _____.

    Application: D. Thinking requires: Hard work
                                                   Time
                                                   Research

Solomon said: "For as he thinks within himself, so he is." Proverbs 23:7
Paul said: " Finally brethren, whatever is true, whatever is honorable, whatever is right, whatever is pure, whatever is lovely, whatever is of good repute…let your mind dwell on these things." Philippians 4:8
Peter said: "Therefore, gird your minds for action…I Peter 1:13

II. Teenagers are _____ about a world of peace, the church, the family, and as a result, _____. (i.e. parents)
    A. They have the mentality, "the grass is greener on the other side of the fence.
       Application: B. Their criticisms should not be
                                 taken _____, but they should not go
                                 _____.
    C. When it comes to people, no one is _____. We should show _____ without _____. We should be _____ rather than _____ when people fail us.

Acts 17:11, the believers were, "examining the Scriptures daily to see whether these things were so."
I Cor 3:7, "So then neither the one who plants nor the one who waters is anything, but God who cares causes the growth."
Proverbs 27:5, 6 "Better is open rebuke than love concealed. Faithful are the wounds of a friend, but deceitful are the kisses of an enemy." _____.

Theodore Roosevelt said: "It is not the critic who counts; not the man who points out how the strong man stumbled or where the doer of deeds could have done better. The credit belongs to the man who is actually in the arena; whose face is marred by dust and sweat and blood; who strives valiantly; who errs, and comes short again and again, because there is no effort without error and shortcoming; who does actually try to do the deed; who knows the great enthusiasm, the great devotion and spends himself in a worthy cause; who, at his worst, if he fails, at least fails while daring greatly. Far better is it to dare mighty things, to win glorious triumphs, even though checkered by failure, than to rank with those poor spirits who neither enjoy nor suffer much because they live in the gray twilight that knows neither victory nor defeat."

III. Teenagers are _____.
   A. They argue _____ _____ _____ _____ _____.
      Application:
      1. They need help in distinguishing between arguing as ____ _____
         ____ _____ or an exercise _____ _____ _____
         _____.

      2. We should attempt to remove _____ _____
         _____, while giving them opportunity to argue.
      3. Parents/adults are threatened when teens begin to _____ _____
         _____.

   B. Adults tend to be argumentative, especially when their teenager _____
      _____.
      1. People do have questions!
      2. Our reaction: argue w/them or prefer arguing with each other, or we give them pre-recorded answers to questions they haven't asked.

I Peter 3:15, "always being ready to make a defense to everyone who asks you to give an account for the hope that is in you, yet with gentleness and reverence."

IV. Teenagers are _____ - _____
   A. Now that teenagers can think about thinking, they can think about what goes on not
      only ____ _____ _____, but also ____ _____ _____
      ____ _____.
   B. They assume that everyone around them is concerned about the same thing their
      concerned about…namely, _____!
      1. This is called an _____ _____.
      2. Teens feel that they are _____ ____ _____.
      3. Everyone is concerned about their _____ and _____.

Application: C. What can adults do?
      1. Be more sensitive about _____ _____.
      2. Adults can help by avoiding _____ _____and _____.
      3. As teens grow older, their concern w/the imaginary audience
         _____.
      4. Don't ever point out _____ _____.
      5. Avoid _____
   D. Adults can make others self-conscious
      1. We make others feel self-conscious. How? Labels!
         a. _____ _____-Choleric, Melancholy, Phlegmatic, Sanguine
         b. _____ _____- dispensationalist, pre-tribulationist, Calvinist, Fundamentalist, neo-evangelist.
         c. Negative _____stereotypical labels
         d. Negative _____stereotypical labels

FOUNDATIONS OF YOUTH MINISTRY

      e. _____ _____
  2. The problem with labels:
     a. They can be _____.
     b. Teenagers tend to _____ _____ or _____ to their labels.

Proverbs 12:17-23, "A truthful witness gives honest testimony, but a false witness tells lies. Reckless words pierce like a sword, but the tongue of the wise brings healing. Truthful lips endure forever, but a lying tongue lasts only a moment. There is deceit in the hearts of those who plot evil, but joy for those who promote peace. No harm befalls the righteous, but the wicked have their fill of trouble. The Lord detests lying lips, but he delights in men who are truthful. A prudent man keeps his knowledge to himself, but the heart of fools blurts out folly."

V.   Teenagers tend to be _____.
    A. They feel that everything that happens to them is unique and original.
      1. "No one has it as bad as me."
      2. "It can't happen to me."
Application: B. What can adults do?
      1. Adults can help by pointing out how other people are _____.
      2. We can learn from other people's _____.

Ted Engtrom writes, "Cripple him, and you have a Sir Walter Scott. Lock him in a prison cell, and you have a John Bunyan. Bury him in the snows of Valley Forge, and you have a George Washington. Raise him in abject poverty, and you have an Abraham Lincoln. Strike him down with infantile paralysis, and he becomes Franklin Roosevelt. Burn him so severely that doctors say he'll never walk again and you have a Glenn Cunningham-who set the world's one mile record in 1934. Deafen him and you have discrimination, and you have a Booker T. Washington, a Marian Anderson, a George Washington Carver...call him a slow learner, 'retarded', and write him off as uneducable, and you have an Albert Einstein."

VI.   Teenagers have difficulty _____ _____.
    A. When teens are forced to make decisions, they come up with choices that seem _____.
      1. _____, usually opposite of parents choice.
      2. _____, reason why they like fast food joints.
Application: B. The difference
      1. The difference here between adults and teens in decision making is _____.
      2. Need to give guidance in the decision making process.
    B. Making decisions
      1. Is there any _____ or _____ from the Scriptures?
      2. What are other people saying, especially your _____ or at the very minimum, _____ _____ who have your best interest at heart?

FOUNDATIONS OF YOUTH MINISTRY

      3. Are there any _____ from the Holy Spirit?
      4. What would be the most spiritually _____ decision?
      5. Do _____ line up with the previous questions?
      6. Are there any negative or harmful _____ _____?
      7. Once you've made the decision, ___ ___ _____ ___ _____?

Joshua was a decision maker, "Now fear the Lord and serve him with all faithfulness. Throw away the gods of your forefathers worshipped beyond the River and in Egypt, and serve the Lord. But if serving the Lord seems undesirable to you, then choose this day whom you will serve, whether the gods your forefathers served beyond the River, or the gods of the Amortize, in whose land you are living. But as for me and my household, we will serve the Lord." Joshua 24:14, 15

VII.   Teenagers appear to be _____.
       A. Teens are _____ about their _____, but often fail in _____ _____ _____ that go along with them.

      Application: B. Teens need to engage in _____ _____, the application of their faith.

VIII.   Teenagers can be _____/_____.
       A. Moving from _____ _____ to a _____ _____.

      B. Because teens value their _____, the idea of a personal God seems great…God keeps _____!

Conclusion: Matthew 18:1-6 "Becoming like a little child"

Vanishing Markers

I. Biblical Markers
   A. _____
   B. _____
   C. _____

II. Markers
   A. The _____ on life's way
   B. Personally _____
   C. Accompanied by _____ _____
   D. Signs of _____
   E. Involves new _____, new _____, and new _____
   F. Helps a young person become aware of progress toward _____
   G. _____ for the future.

III. Markers Disappearance
   A. Should be _____ about markers disappearance.
   B. Markers protect teens _____ stress and _____ the stress they must encounter
   C. Markers supply _____, _____, and _____ teens from making _____ decisions.
   D. Adolescents want to be like the next _____ age group, not like the _____ age group
   E. Examples:
   _____
   _____
   _____
   _____
   _____

IV. Markers that have disappeared
   A. _____ markers
   B. _____ markers
      - _____
      - _____
      - _____
      - _____
      - _____
   C. _____ markers

- _____
- _____

D. _____ markers
1. Like the young of any species, our young require the care, protection, and guidance of _____
2. Modern tendency is to _____ every type of depravity or evil to children.
3. It is a _____ assumption that this will prepare them to live successful, virtuous lives (that a bad experience is the best preparation for a bad experience…the reverse is true…a _____ experience is the best preparation for a _____ experience. (_____).
4. It is 'cheaper' to build a _____ at the top of a cliff than a _____ at the bottom.
5. Making information available to children, whether they comprehend it or not, _____ its value as a marker for those who are more prepared for it…namely older _____
6. Examples:
    - _____
    - _____
    - _____
    - _____

V. Conclusion
A. We cannot and should not prevent young people from learning about the dangers of the world.
B. When young people are portrayed as being fully competent to deal with these complex adult issues they are discouraged from seeking adult…
1. _____
2. _____
3. _____ they so desperately need.

Overview of Adolescent Development

While there is no such thing as a typical teenager, there are general characteristics of teenagers that depict what might be "norm" for a teenager as he or she move through the teenage years.

Physical

Early Adolescence (12-13 years old)	Middle Adolescence (14-15 years old)	Late Adolescence (16-18 years old)
_____ are rapid and dramatic, i.e., growth	Physical changes have _____ for girls; boys may still be changing rapidly	_____ is almost fully developed
_____ is lacking; tiredness and short attention span are common	Advanced development of 2nd sexual characteristics	Boys have caught up with girls _____
_____ ; hands and feet are large in proportion to rest of body	Develop _____ (particularly males)	Majority have reached _____
Begins to show physical signs of sexual maturity; emergence of 2nd sexual characteristics	Active and energetic	Express a strong interest in _____
Girls are usually more _____ than boys, entering puberty up to 2 years earlier	Tends to experiment with alcohol or drugs	May fall victim to _____
Most have super-human _____	Increased _____ and _____	Some are sexually experienced
Boys: _____	_____ (males require 3400 calories daily/females require 2800 calories to sustain normal growth)	
Girls: Monthly Cycle begins, rounding of pelvis, breast development, _____		
Skin becomes coarser and more porous		
Glands produce oily secretion contributing to vulnerability to _____		
Extremities of the body are first to reach adult size; out _____		
Growing pains		

Emotional

Early Adolescence (12-13 years old)	Middle Adolescence (14-15 years old)	Late Adolescence (16-18 years old)
Begins to develop personal identity and sense of self	Begins to form personal relationships	Feels confidence and security with own identity
Self-conscious and egocentric; but gaining more confidence	Less ego centric; learns how to give of themselves and receive from others	Sometimes sentimental
Enthusiastic	Often enjoys arguments	Can put others' needs ahead of their own
Still depends on parents, but desire for independence is increasing	Feels intense need to begin to separate from parents	Recognizes the need to take more personal responsibility
Fluctuate between _____ and _____	Self-assurance can mask _____ and _____	Usually friendly towards _____
Expresses a positive sense of humor	Seeks _____ for being good in some activity	_____ and _____ assume greater prominence
Worry about how body looks	Thought become less egocentric (can think from the other person's point-of-view)	Stabilization of identity
Strong fear of _____	The loss of idealism is manifested by _____, _____, _____, and _____.	Deepening of interest, including _____, _____, _____
Praise is not really accepted, though some adults have extraordinary influence by a _____	All areas of _____ _____ show an upspring (i.e., death by car accident; suicide; homicide; overdoses; depression, etc.)	Expansion of caring
Self-centered	Emotions _____ in power (tend to exaggerate)	Able to handle _____ like spouse, parent, student, employee, etc.
Areas of high stress include: _____, _____, _____, _____	_____ shows up as aimless, anger depression	

Social

Early Adolescence (12-13 years old)	Middle Adolescence (14-15 years old)	Late Adolescence (16-18 years old)
Places great value on _____ ; wants to fit in with crowd	Focus moves from same-sex friendships to _____ ; dates in _____ .	Desire meaningful relationships with _____ , _____
Looks to attach to a few close friends; often "cliquish"	Stays with _____	Dating is frequent
Can be _____ and have _____	May join a group with social beliefs or values that _____ _____	Personal relationships show _____ _____ ; many date one partner exclusively
Develops _____ and identifies _____	Sometimes rebel against _____	Some are sexually active
Most comfortable in small groups of trusted friends of the same sex	May become very protective of personal possessions	Driver's license and graduation will be rites of passage
Experiments with appropriate behaviors; tests limits		Most work part-time, resulting in discretionary income
Peer group is prominent	More disciplined in choosing friends (not just from same neighborhood or classroom)	More self-reliant because they are more sure of "who" they are
	Strong need for belonging	Less susceptible to peer manipulation
	Get together for fear of isolation as much a desire for friendship	Relationship with elders are sought

Intellectual

Early Adolescence (12-13 years old)	Middle Adolescence (14-15 years old)	Late Adolescence (16-18 years old)
Wants to see _____, and less willing to accept others' beliefs (_____)	Becomes capable of more _____ and _____.	Becomes increasingly involved with _____.
Begins to think _____ but usually views issues in terms of black and white answers; increasingly uses reason and logic	Can ask _____	Begins to focus on _____.
Grows in ability to make decisions based on personal values	More _____ and _____ about belief systems	Develops ability to _____ _____; can process possibilities
Makes decisions that often are idealistic and sometimes _____		Makes better and more mature decisions
Learning the roles of _____ and _____		Might be able to resolve conflicts _____
Significant amount of curiosity about _____.	They understand that mental conclusions result from _____	
Difficult to teach because they think they know it all	Critical age for adjustment in school	
Easy to teach because they believe in authority	Household relationships improve due to increased ability to "read" parent(s)	

Spiritual

Early Adolescence (12-13 years old)	Middle Adolescence (14-15 years old)	Late Adolescence (16-18 years old)
Generally _____ to making a decision about a relationship with Christ	Searches for what _____ says about what is and isn't OK	Shows ability to demonstrate _____ _____ to a relationship with Christ
More able to make _____ _____	May experience _____ about relationships with or thoughts about opposite sex	_____ and _____ are tested and challenged
Develops a more sensitive view of _____	May experience _____ with desire to stop some behavior and the apparent inability to do so (like pornography)	_____ and _____ about how others feel and think
Begins to develop personal _____		Becomes interested in _____
Usually mirror parents _____ _____ initially		Ask questions and expresses concern about their _____ _____ (assurance of salvation)
Responds to needs of others; more aware of _____ _____		Is increasingly able to apply _____ _____ (principle) to life and is able to grasp deeper spiritual concepts

FOUNDATIONS OF YOUTH MINISTRY

Irrational Beliefs During Adolescence

1. Necessary to be approved of by everyone including parents, teachers, neighbors, and all their peers.

   Response:_____
   _____
   _____.

2. One should be thoroughly competent, adequate, and achieving.

   Response:_____
   _____
   _____.

3. Certain people are bad or wicked simply because they are different and should be punished for their differences.

   Response:_____
   _____
   _____.

4. It is awful or catastrophic when things are not exactly the way one wants them to be.

   Response:_____
   _____
   _____
   _____
   _____.

5. They should worry about other peoples' problems.

   Response: _____
   _____
   _____

6. Happiness is externally controlled and people have little or no ability to control the things which bring them joy or cause them sorrow.

Response: _____
_____
_____.

7. Any attempt to equal the achievements of my peers is out of the question.

Response:_____
_____
_____.

8. Everything in life is a win-lose perspective.

Response: _____
_____
_____.

9. People who believe differently are viewed as having moral inferiority's rather than merely differences in behavior.

Response: _____
_____
_____.

10. One has the right to be free from discomfort and to glide through life with only minimum frustration.

Response: _____
_____
_____.

FOUNDATIONS OF YOUTH MINISTRY

Why We Misperceive the Nature of Adolescence

1. _____ of superficial signs of non-conformity

2. Mass media _____

3. _____ from samples of deviant adolescents

4. _____ on the biological determination of heterosexual behavior

5. _____ prophecy

6. Lack of interest in _____ form, ritual, and participation

7. The ability to manage the _____ granting of adult roles and responsibilities

What Adults Can Do:

1. Say, "_____"
2. Deal with _____, not pressure
3. Be _____
4. _____ with it at the time
5. Don't _____ too much
6. Talk
7. Know their _____
8. Don't try to be perfect
9. Parents who succeed with teens have a sense of _____
10. Instill _____ in them for the future

"Extra Grace Required" Teenagers

I. Ministering to Young People With Disabilities

   A. All God's children are given _____ _____ to use in his service, even those with the most profound disabilities. I Corinthians 12

   B. Institute a youth _____ _____
   -include youth with disabilities in planning and decision-making

   C. They want to be _____ just like everyone else; don't focus on the ways that they are _____

   D. Encourage compassion and _____ in all group members by finding or creating _____ for them to help people with many different needs

   E. Be aware of all _____ _____ that those students with physical disabilities might have and work to remove them

   F. Allow youth with disabilities to participate _____ in all youth group activities by _____ activities on an individual basis only when it's absolutely necessary

   G. Ask youth group members who have disabilities (if they're receptive to the idea) to help "teach" the group the best ways to _____ and _____ with those with disabilities, highlighting especially the ways they would like to be treated.

   H. Be sure to be aware of, and prepared to help with, any special-care needs a youth group member with disabilities may have, especially if he or she will be away from home for an _____ period of time, such as at a retreat.

   I. _____ yourself as well as the rest of your youth group. Do some research about the type of disability a youth group member has. This information may help you to work with and care for him or her more effectively.

   J. Examine your own _____ of disabilities and people who have them

   K. Search Scripture to discover God's view of disabilities. A few passages to start with are _____; _____; _____; _____; _____, _____; _____; _____.

FOUNDATIONS OF YOUTH MINISTRY

    L.   Strive to model and encourage _____, _____ _____ among youth group members

    M.   For those with more involved disabilities, you may want to use a _____ _____, in which able-bodied youth group members volunteer to "come along-side" those with disabilities, offering friendship and help and encouragement when it's needed.

II.   Connecting With Youth Who Have Anger Issues

    A. Help teenagers identify the _____ of their anger
    B. _____ _____
    C. Model Christ-like _____
    D. _____ _____. Youth who are angry tend to sabotage relationships with people who try to get close to them. The deeper the relationship develops, the more fearful they become.
    E. _____. Angry teenagers require adults who will stay with them long enough to repair their distorted parental image. It takes adults who are very secure in their own identity in Christ to unconditionally love kids through this difficult period; people who realize that the attacks aren't personal, but represent a lifetime of rejection. But having such relationships opens young people to being able to trust others as well. And as a result, the anger thermometer can begin to drop a couple of notches.
    F. Avoid speaking _____ about a young person's _____. Even when it seems clear that a teenager's mother or father is to blame, the parents are still the parents. The parental bond is so strong that our negative words only put the young person in the awkward position of having to oppose us in order to defend the parent.
    G. _____ about anger from the Scriptures.
    H. Teach teenagers to deal with _____. Ephesians 4:26b
    I. _____ your own anger. Proverbs 15:1
    J. Help teenagers move toward _____

III. Ministering to Young People in Blended Families

   A. It's important to realize that family blending occurs whenever two or more _____ (or _____ _____) are combined. Biological families get a chance to slowly grow a family life. Blended teenagers come with a prepackaged history and have to learn, accept, and eventually promote a new life story.
   B. Meditate on _____. Joseph, at this moment in his life, was realizing his own blended-family situation.
   C. Don't assume that blended-family children are "_____."
   D. Encourage family _____ in your group.
   E. Model your own _____. Everyone has areas in their past that are unlike a traditional family background. Talk openly about these unique characteristics.
   F. Either directly or indirectly, _____ your youth group to resemble a family.
   G. Realize that it's normal for members of blended families to feel like they're between _____ _____ _____.
   H. _____ regularly with the adults immediately responsible for these special teenagers. Don't find yourself in the position of being a _____ for warring parents.
   I. Blended teenagers need a healthy idea of _____.
   J. Understand that people in blended families are frequently caught in _____ _____. The teenager may get involved with youth group one week and be absent the next because of a second parent's schedule. _____ is totally lacking in their lives.
   K. Strive to convey the thought that blended-family situations are _____ _____, in fact they can be tough, but they're very doable.
   L. Be ready to recommend resources or have them available for "_____ _____" or "_____ _____."

Postmodernism

FOUNDATIONS OF YOUTH MINISTRY

Post Modern Times

There is decisive shift in the U.S. perspective of truth. When culture changes, what should be the Christian Reaction?

> DOCTRINE never changes
> PRINCIPLES are eternal
> METHODS will change
> The BOTTOMLINE in issues is knowing when to stand and what to update,
> i.e. grounded on the ROCK but updated for today.

I. The Two Models of Truth
   A. Model #1
      1. Truth is defined by God for _____; it is _____ and _____.
      2. Acknowledges God as _____ in the universe. The origin and repository for _____; the author and judge of right and wrong.
   B. Model #2
      1. Truth is defined by the _____; it is _____ and _____.
      2. Places the _____ as central and in control; _____ - _____. There is no _____ truth; truth is _____ to the individual and to the _____ _____.

"If there is no absolute moral standard, then one cannot say in a final sense that anything is right or wrong. By absolute we mean that which always applies, that which provides a final or ultimate standard. There must be an absolute if there are to be morals, and there must be an absolute if there are to be real values. If there is no absolute beyond man's ideas, then there is no final appeal to judge between individuals and groups whose moral judgments conflict. We are merely left with conflicting opinions."

- **Francis Schaeffer**

FOUNDATIONS OF YOUTH MINISTRY

II. What is the focus of this issue?
    A. _____. The standard is God as revealed in the Bible.
    B. _____ _____. There is a measure of right and wrong.
    C. _____ _____. is always right for all people in all places for all time. This is based on the nature of God: If HE is all powerful, then nothing is greater than HE. If HE is all wise, then nothing is smarter than HE or knows what is right or wrong better than HE. If HE is eternal, then nothing came before or created God.
    D. _____. If there is no standard of right and wrong then what is sin?

III. What does AT/AM do for me?
    A. Basis for _____
    B. Individual _____
    C. _____ in life
    D. Defining life - Character
    E. Public _____
    F. _____
    G. _____ Restraint

FOUNDATIONS OF YOUTH MINISTRY

Truth

There have always been wild and rebellious kids who would go off the track and do something wrong. But they knew where the track was and what was wrong. Many of today's youth don't seem to know right from wrong.

I. Today in America
    A. _____ teens will attempt suicide [1]
    B. 2,795 teenage girls will become _____ [1]
    C. _____ teenage girls get an abortion [1]
    D. _____ teens will use drugs for the first time [1]
    E. _____ kids bring guns or other weapons to school
    F. 3,610 teens are _____; 80 _____
    G. _____ teens drop out of high school
    H. _____ teens will run away [1]
    I. Teens now account _____ of all sexually transmitted diseases
    J. Over _____ of all teens use alcohol or drugs

II. Living on the Moral Edge
    A. Christian parents (or pastors or youth leaders) number one fear these days is that they will not be able to _____ their _____ on to the next generation
    B. A survey of over 3,700 youth _____ _____ throughout the U.S. and Canada revealed that our youth are living on a _____ _____, closer to _____ than we ever imagined.

        1. In the past three months...
           a. _____ of our kids lied to a parent, teacher, or other adult
           b. _____ lied to their parents
           c. _____ watched MTV at least once a week
           d. _____ cheated on an exam
           e. _____ smoked a cigarette or used another tobacco product
           f. _____ tried to physically hurt someone
           g. _____ had gotten drunk
           h. _____ had used illegal, non-prescription drugs

        2. Our _____ _____ are not much better than _____-_____ _____ in virtually every area we cited, but...

---

[1] http://www.vpp.com/teenhelp/

FOUNDATIONS OF YOUTH MINISTRY

      a. Too many are involved in _____ _____
      b. Too many are _____, _____, _____ _____
      c. Too many are hurting other people, _____ _____ _____ _____

> "We may be one of the few societies in the world that finds itself incapable of passing on its moral teachings to young people."
> - philosophy professor

III. An Issue of Truth

"I believe that one of the primary reasons this generation is setting new records for dishonesty, disrespect, sexual promiscuity, violence, suicide, and other pathologies, is because they have lost their moral underpinning; their foundational belief in morality and truth has been eroded." Anonymous

  A Truth has become a matter of _____; morality has been replaced by _____ _____

  B. "There is one thing a _____ can be absolutely certain of: almost every student entering the university believes, or says he believes, that truth is _____."
     -Allan Bloom, <u>The Closing of the American Mind</u>

  C. Our society has so emphasized _____ _____ and _____ that practically an entire generation of young people have rejected an _____ _____ for right and wrong.

V. Absolute Truth
    A. That which is _____ for all _____, for all _____, for all _____

    B. Absolute truth is truth that is _____, _____ and _____

    C. If our children are going to learn how to determine right from wrong, they must know what truths are _____ and _____.
        Proverbs 26:3
        2 Timothy 3:16
        Psalm 19

> *When our youth are equipped with the proper "truth view," based on a proper World View, they will be better able to identify what truths are absolute and what makes them absolute...and they will have a fighting chance to make the right choices.*

Our Response to this Culture:

OFFENDED	_____
DELIGHTED	_____
DISTRESSED	_____

Unbalanced Immersionist
(loses his _____)

[Radical Difference]

          [Radical Identification]

Δ

Unbalanced Rejectionist
(loses his _____)

          [Radical Identification]

[Radical Difference]

Δ

Balanced Communicator
(_____ observation and _____ participation)

[Radical Difference]   [Radical Identification]

Δ

Take the media...please!

Media is _____. It's the _____ that makes the difference.

Kids encounter content without assessing its value.
- _____
- _____
- _____
- _____

When it comes to choosing content, most young people mimic the behavior of a two-year-old, _____ _____ ____ _____ _____.

Young people _____ what adults _____.
Given our reputation on _____ and _____, adults will continue to make what people will buy.

Our job is to train kids to make _____ choices about content.

Need to develop critical media skills
-do not look at the _____ _____
-attempt to _____ from it
-need to have a tight woven _____ for our minds
-what and why does this _____ with you
-try to see the _____ or _____ message being presented
-need to develop the ability to "_____ ____ _____"
-development discernment in the _____ of popular media culture
-use the media on your _____, not the media's terms

Reaching Teens in a Post Modern World

1. _____, not monologue. Talk, don't preach.
No easy or pat answers.
Use _____ _____ stories.
Share _____ _____ stories.
Tell _____ stories.
2. _____
They need to experience God for themselves
Use the _____.
_____ gatherings.
Music.
Needs to be _____ in nature.
Explain the _____ behind worship elements.
3. _____
Small Groups
Getaway experiences.
Be with them.
4. Talk the right talk. (Can be _____ and _____)

5. Walk the talk.
6. Witness where we live. (Promote _____ involvement, not just in our world but in our neighborhood.)

7. Practice long term _____.

8. Live a modest lifestyle. (Don't be caught in a _____ culture or buy into the belief that the more you have, the happier you'll be.)

9. Reclaim a Christian sense of time. (Don't be over _____. Slow down.)

10. Know their culture. (_____, _____, _____)

11. Make a deliberate attempt to _____ them into the church.

12. Develop and nurture _____ (with _____; with caring _____; with _____ young people; with Jesus Christ).

Family And Adolescents

Family Friendly Ministry

Today more than any point in the past, the youth leader's ministry must _____ the parents and the _____ _____ _____. The trend is toward a _____ ministry. Youth leaders across the nation are involved in such activities as _____/_____ _____ _____, _____ _____ _____, providing resources, and being a _____ _____ for many family issues.

Remember the primary responsibility of raising a child rest with the parents: (Joel 1:3; Det. 6). However in some cases of broken homes, unsaved parents, the youth worker is needed to fill this gap (Gal. 6:2).

"The youth workers role in a students spiritual growth is helpful, the parents role is essential." Doug Fields

1. Biblical Basis for this ministry:
   a.
   b.
   c.
   d.
   e.
   f.
   g.
   h.

Ideal as a youth leader, you should be _____ the truths taught at home. _____ the parents, not being one!

2. Why this need now?
   a.
   b.

"Every album you kids play, every concert they attend, every television show they watch each one is like a step-dad temporarily taking over your role of teacher, coach and friend" **Joe White**

3. New Trends:
   a.
   b.
   c.
   d.
   e.

FOUNDATIONS OF YOUTH MINISTRY

4. Parent Part of the Problem:
   a.
   b.
   c.
   d.
   e.
   f.
   g.
   h.

"It is better to lose a few books and a few hours of reading now — or few business opportunities, a few overtime hours, or a few ministry opportunities — than to lose a child later"

5. Conclusion:
   a. Parents must be _____, _____, and _____ connected to their kids.
   b. Help parents understand what _____ _____ and then set the _____ _____.

"We have grown in numbers, wealth, and power as no other nation has grown, but we have forgotten God. We have forgotten the gracious hand that preserved us in peace and multiplied and enriched and strengthened us. We have vainly imagined that all these blessings were produced by some superior virtue and wisdom of our own…Intoxicated with unbroken success, we have become too self-sufficient to feel the necessity of redeeming and preserving grace, too proud to pray to the God that made us." **—Abraham Lincoln**

Family Friendly Ministry

A _____, _____, and _____ church
A parent-_____ system
A strong educational ministry for _____
A dynamic _____ ministry

Parents are often _____.
Parents are scared of the _____.
Parents love their _____.
Parents are nervous about the _____.
Parents are _____.
Parents wish they had more _____.
Parents are often _____.
Parents don't always "have it all together."
Parents want to be taken _____.
Parents, on the inside, often still think of themselves as being in _____ _____.

Five Cries of Parents

To _____ themselves and their adolescents.
To _____ a close and supportive family life.
To see _____ behavior and purpose developing in their children.
To know how a shared _____ can be experienced by their family.
To know where to turn for help in _____ _____.

Why Parent/Family Ministry is Such Hard Work

Youth workers have to consider the needs of the _____ _____ group while parents focus on their own _____.
Youth workers might have the inside scoop on family _____.
Youth workers are too busy already and don't have time and energy for more _____.
Youth workers often love being needed. When we're _____, we often shut parents out.
Parents may feel _____ when their kids are drawn to the youth workers.
Parents may not _____ young youth workers without teenagers of their own.
Parents may think they're hiring a _____. *(Beware of going into a ministry Setting where the calendar is king and your ministry is evaluated by the number of Activities you can pull off each month.)*
Parents may experience a _____ associated with needing help.

Family Ministry Paradigm

1. _____ (The youth worker recognizes that each adolescent has a family context that matters. The range of family systems must be factored into planning and programming.)

2. _____ (The youth worker takes every opportunity to present parents and the family in a positive way through attitude, teaching, application, and modeling.)

3. _____ (The youth worker communicates carefully with parents about every detail of youth ministry activities and listens carefully to their input and feedback.)

4. _____ (The youth worker looks for ways to encourage and bless individual parents in their relationships with their adolescent children.)

5. _____ (The youth worker finds ways to facilitate relationships between parents for their mutual benefit and encouragement.)

6. _____ (The youth worker provides parents with resources to strengthen and equip them in their parenting role.)

7. _____ (The youth worker finds appropriate ways for parents to participate.)

8. _____ (The youth worker teaches parents of teens in legitimate areas of expertise.)

9. _____ (The youth worker is seen as a partner with a growing number of parents.)

An Effective Parenting Matrix

Parenting Models

Authoritative Parent	Permissive Parent	Authoritarian Parent
Stresses control	Stresses support	Stresses control
AND _____	NO _____	NOT _____

Parent-Teen Relationship Models

Companionship	Extreme Affection	Extreme Control
Open communication between parents & children	Suffocating affection	Little _____ _____ between generations
Fair _____	Youth is afraid. _____ will hurt parent	Poor communication with strong discipline

Family Type

Translucent	Transparent	Opaque
Family is _____ with society but has own distinctions	Family has no _____ from general social values	Family completely _____ from society
Parents _____ outside world fairly	Parents offer no _____ of outside world	Family is right; all outside sources are considered _____ or _____
Family is not _____ to other values	Family has no _____ family values	Family ascribes faith only to those who fully _____

32

FOUNDATIONS OF YOUTH MINISTRY

Parenting Practices

More than _____ _____ adolescents call North America home.

In _____, six years after the World War II ended, the day after _____ _____, a tide swept over the US.

That was the day the first wave of _____ _____ broke on the schools of _____. Kindergarten classes, which averaged about ____ students in _____, had more than __ in ____. As a result:
- Teachers now spent a large part of their _____ on crowd _____.
- Students became _____ _____. The most _____ students learned to _____ which points in the teacher's lectures were _____.
- _____ replaced _____ overnight.
- _____ was gradually replaced by _____ _____ testing.
- Classroom discussion was _____ by a few students at the front of the classroom.

In the fall of _____, over _____ million children enrolled for school, the _____ number in US history. (NBC News, August 16, 1999)

In 1970, _____ _____ (one in every three marriages). The _____ _____ of the marriages that ended was not quite _____ years.
From 1975 to 1995, there were roughly _____ _____ _____ for every _____ marriages.
In 1997, about _____ _____ children (one in four) under the age of 18, lived with only _____ _____.

The toxicity in our culture can be measured by:
-
-
-
-
-
-
-
-

33

Danger Signs?

-
-
-
-
-
-
-

There's a lot of evidence that kids _____ _____ _____ before they listen to their _____.

The truth is, kids _____ first toward _____ people who _____ and _____ them and with whom they feel _____. If no one like that is around, then they look to _____ for _____, _____, and _____. *The downside* is that what many adults care about isn't good for kids-or adults for that matter.

Controlling

Controlling begins with the _____ that I know you _____ than you know _____.

Controllers assume kids will make the _____ _____.

Most people mean no _____. Their goal is to head off _____ consequences.

The underlying message of controlling: _____ _____ _____ _____.

You need me for the most _____ matters. *"You'd lose you mind if I didn't hang it on the door every morning. Never forget that. And by the way, have a good day at school."*

Controlling fosters _____ instead of encouraging _____ _____.

Controllers insist on looking after every detail like what to _____, what to _____, how to _____, when to _____ and _____.

Controllers assume they know what other people _____ and _____.

Discovering instead of Controlling

Discoverers seek _____ only his child can provide but won't _____ unless asked.

(A good question is one to which you don't have the answer.)

Most questions are _____ and kids get used to being _____ and _____ _____ by adults.

After a while, most kids learn to be _____, to avoid _____ _____. They learn the art of _____ and _____ _____ _____ _____.

-By asking good questions and listening carefully to the answers will help you discover the weak spots in your child's skills.

-When you take your youngster _____ _____ to ask questions you can't already answer, you're preparing him to let you in on a whole lot of other, deeper stuff.

-Your child won't _____ expect that all adults are out to make them look stupid.

Questions
Why do you think controlling is so attractive?
How do you feel when someone thinks he can read your mind?
Can you think of three questions you can ask a kid that you don't already know the answer to?

Fixing
The line between _____ and _____ is severely blurred for most kids because, by and large, they don't understand the general _____ of _____ and _____. Adults in their lives come up behind them and _____ when they mess up. Idle _____ and _____ idle _____ complicate this.
Many of us rescue them from the _____ of their _____ and _____.

Our kids can't afford to have us fix things for them. They may not be able to survive it. What they need is honesty, accountability, and decisive action.

Cooperating instead of Fixing
The fixer follows an expedient path to _____-_____ _____.
Three questions for the cooperator:
1. _____ _____ _____ _____ _____? (What matters is hearing what the kids thinks he/she experienced.)
2. _____ _____ _____ _____ _____ _____? (The young person is ready to assign meaning to the experience. It calls for an assessment of decision-making skills and wishful thinking.)
3. _____ _____ _____ _____ _____ _____ _____ _____ _____ (or avoid this failure?) (Now the young person can take strategic action to repeat success or avoid failure.)

The beauty about cooperating is you don't have to do it forever. Eventually, you can help your young person see what you've been doing (and why and how you do it). Then, in most situations, they can take over the process themselves.

Questions
Are you a fixer and why?
Anything significant stand out here and why?

Bossing

_____ likes to be around bossy people. Bosses know too much. They know how to do it- whatever it is- _____ than anyone else.

Partnering instead of Bossing

A partner:
_____
_____
_____
_____

A boss turns into a Partner when:
_____
_____
_____

Asking for help and really meaning it, spells the end of _____.
Partners place more value on _____ than _____.

When we partner, our young person:
becomes a _____ not just an _____
learns new skills that prepare them for the future

Questions

Is there a bossy person in your life? How do you feel about being bossed?
Is there a partner in your life? How do you feel about that person?
If you are prone to bossing, when are you most likely to do so? Why?
What might keep you from partnering instead of bossing?

Demanding

Demanding adults routinely criticize children for not being _____ _____. Their _____ are too high and too immediate for children to live up to. Their standards are _____ for the simple reason that they are _____ _____.
There is nothing wrong with high standards if they're appropriate.
Because kids look _____-_____, adults demand _____-_____ perceptions and skills from them.

So when adults are impatient in their demands, kids often bluff by:
_____
_____
_____ _____
_____ _____ _____

FOUNDATIONS OF YOUTH MINISTRY

In a reasonably healthy environment, kids will rise to life's challenges. They want to learn and grow because _____ _____ _____ are stimulating and fun. But this is retarded in an overly demanding environment in which failure isn't tolerated.
If failure isn't acceptable, trial and error is thrown out as a learning strategy.
Then kids resort to:

_____

_____ _____

_____ _____ _____

Affirming instead of Demanding

Affirming looks at a behavior or a process and responds with a constructive, concrete endorsement: "You did well" "I admire your work" "Congratulations on a job well done"
Affirming takes place independent of outcomes.

Parents are in a unique position to celebrate the learning process by:
_____ _____ _____
_____ _____ as the context for correction and training
_____ _____ _____ _____

(Be cautious about praising things that children _____ _____ ____ _____ _____, i.e. You're so pretty; You're so tall; What big beautiful eyes you have! Kids who get praise for things outside their control or acts of God, become suspicious of people and nervous about their own worth. Looks do change.)

Questions

Can you recall an adult who demanded the wrong things from you? How did you feel?
Can you identify ways in which you've been tempted to demand the wrong things from a younger person?
Can you recall an adult who affirmed you?
Have you seen praising substituted for affirming?
What are areas that you can legitimately affirm young people?

Shaming

Shaming is a context where the _____ doesn't necessarily indicate an honest question…"What were you thinking?!" (conveys a message _____ _____)
There's no reason to belittle a kid because he hasn't gotten to the part of the training where he knows better. He doesn't.
Shaming sets kids up for _____ _____ from _____ _____.

The kid is easy picking for anyone who wants to _____ _____.
Children who are shamed grow up to have sick relationships with their parents. They become
_____ _____ and _____.
_____ is the appropriate blush that says _____ _____ _____
_____ and I should make it right.
_____ is a deeper blush that says _____ _____ _____ _____ and I can never be made right.

Respect instead of Shaming
Respect isn't _____ - _____ _____ of any and all behavior.
Respect grows from the acknowledgement that all of us are _____ _____.
Respect acknowledges that what's _____ to one person may not be a bit _____ to someone else.
Shaming is _____. Respect is _____.
To show respect, _____ _____ _____ and _____ _____, whether we agree or not.

Questions
Have you ever been shamed?
Have you ever shamed someone else?
How do you feel toward people who respect you?
How do you feel when you treat a young person with respect?

The Extremes

Controlling
Control says NO before the question is finished.
There's nothing to talk about.
If control is hostile, a kid has a tendency towards:
-
-
-
-
-

Permissiveness
Knows _____ _____
Sets no _____
Kids feel out of control.
The child of permissiveness is likely to be:
-
-
-
-
-

Kids require increasing levels of freedom.
Too much freedom too early is _____.
Appropriate freedom withheld can be _____.
By the time kids reach adolescence, we can be hands off about a lot of things-but _____ _____.
(If we balance _____ with _____, we will always be allowed to be involved with our kids.)
Give kids something _____ _____ _____.
Communicate _____ _____.
Provide appropriate training. (_____, _____, _____, _____)
Create _____ _____. (safe from _____, _____, and _____)
-
-
-

FOUNDATIONS OF YOUTH MINISTRY

Become a _____ _____. (What a pity when a child looks into the eyes of his parents and thinks, "I'd better not go there alone.")

- _____, _____, _____ - _____, _____ are attributes of unsafe people
-
-
-
- if your kid is victimized, _____ _____ _____(find out what your kid thinks happened before you rush into judgment.

Teach kids to take a self-assessment test.(a kind of global positioning)

-

-

-

-

Recovering addicts use an acronym HALT.
Don't let yourself get too:

H
A
L
T

Teach a more sophisticated _____ _____.
Listen, really listen. (don't be guilty of preparing what you're going to say in response.)

Using Curriculum

Biblical Teaching and Curriculum Design

1. Introduction: What is the purpose of your teaching? Is the Gospel of Jesus Christ making an _____ _____ _____? The Bible was not _____ to make you a _____ sinner. If you are not having an _____ with youth, _____ _____?

2. Why teach?

    a. Because Christ _____ _____! Matthew 28:16-20

        1. The Great _____ or _____
        2. The Great Commission was given _____ times
        3. It is simply not an _____

    b. Because the _____ _____ practiced it

        1. _____ – Acts 2:41-47
        2. _____ – Ephesians 4:11-16; 2 Timothy 2:2
        3. _____ – James 3:1-2

THE ROLE OF THE TEACHER
Jesus the Master Model

Jesus was the quintessential teacher. HE provides the teaching _____. He was the ultimate _____ and _____ of teaching, though He never _____ the subject. His _____ modeled the _____.

In the New Testament, there are more than 40 epithets used to describe the person and work of Jesus Christ. Within the gospels, one of the most frequently used designations is _____; it occurs 45 times, _____ 14 (Teacher come from God).

Students of Scripture often study the _____ of the Gospels (_____ _____ _____) but tend to _____ the _____ of the Gospels (_____ _____ _____ _____ _____). We need to remind ourselves that what Christ _____ and what He _____ were _____ inspired by God. He could say in every scene and circumstance of His life, "I always do what pleases Him (John 8:29)."

"He seems to do nothing of Himself which he can possibly delegate to His Creatures. HE commands us to do slowly and blunderingly what He could do perfectly and in the twinkling of an eye...perhaps we do not full realize the problem, so to call it of enabling finite wills to coexist with Omnipotence. It seems to involve at every moment almost a sort of divine abdication." - C.S. Lewis

THE TROUBLE WITH TEACHING

1. John 15:5 — In your opinion, what implication does this verse have for teachers?

2. James 3:1 — What problem is there in being a teacher?

3. Col. 1:28 — What limits does Paul seem to place on his "student body?" What goal does he suggest for every Christian?

4. 2 Peter 3:15-16 — What encouragement do you find for students of the Bible?

5. 1 Cor. 8:1 — What dangers do you find for students in the Bible?

6. 1 Cor. 2:14-3:3 — Problems to anticipate in communicating spiritual truth?

7. 1 Peter 5:8 — Warning given?

Teaching is as easy as _____

I. P

   A. Lesson aims - _____

   B. Lesson Plans - _____

II. I

   A.
      1.
      2.

   B.
      1.
      2.
      3.

III. E

   A.
   B.
   C.

FOUNDATIONS OF YOUTH MINISTRY

LESSON AIMS/ LESSON PLANS / CURRICULUM
Curriculum

Definition:
The materials, aids, helps, information developed and implemented in order to help achieve our goal of teaching youth the life changing truth of Scripture and the subsequent lifestyle that is associated with these truths.
Dr. Lee P. Vukich

The **VISIBLE** part of curriculum
- ➢ _____
- ➢ _____ of the learner
- ➢ Delivery
- ➢ _____ Resources
- ➢ Other learning aids

The **HIDDEN** part
- ➢ _____ - You behave how you believe
- ➢ _____
- ➢ Curriculum Theory
- ➢ _____ - Lesson Aims, Plans
- ➢ Pray
- ➢ Holy Spirit Dependence

Criteria for Evaluation of Adolescent Curriculum

1. Sets forth foundational truths of the Christian faith concerning God, man, creation and redemption.
2. Is compatible with doctrines, positions and convictions we want to teach our youth.
3. Encourages a personal faith in Jesus Christ.
4. Nurtures an ever deepening commitment to Christ.

---

1. Provides a faithful, thorough and accurate record of the Scriptures that is taken from an accepted translation of the original languages and texts.
2. Treats the Bible as inerrant and infallible in all areas to which it speaks.
3. Treats the Bible as relevant for today.
4. Covers an appropriate amount and selection of Bible content for each lesson that is applicable for the age group.
5. Encourages memorization and development of independent Bible study skills.

---

1. The learning objectives are well rounded and suited for the age-group.
2. The objectives are clearly stated and work together toward a specific desired response.
3. Each objective can be met through the lesson content and teaching methods.
4. Each lesson allows for review and builds incrementally on each other toward a stated objective.
5. The objectives can be easily measured and evaluated.

---

1. Lesson content is relevant to the particular needs, interests, and abilities of the age group.
2. Learning activities/methodologies are varied and stimulating.
3. All activities reinforce the stated learning objectives.
4. Lesson plans take into consideration differences in learning styles and abilities among students at the same age- level.
5. Students are furnished with lesson plans/outlines or handouts that allow them to be involved during class time, i.e., writing things down, answering questions, etc.
6. Student is furnished with take-home materials that help reinforce the lesson.
7. Lessons are reinforced with devotional and memorization materials to be used by the
student between lessons.

Has a well-organized section or separate book of teacher helps.
The teacher helps are genuinely helpful for both experienced and new teachers.
1. The teacher helps and aids are plentiful, visually appealing and well-integrated into the lesson plan.
2. Helps allow/encourage teachers to expand and grow in their own faith and teaching skills.

1. The visuals and graphics are colorful and attractive.
2. The paper and print are of high quality.
3. The materials are reasonably priced

CURRICULUM
What is it?

DEFINITION OF CURRICULUM

THE MATERIALS, AIDS AND INFORMATION DEVELOPED AND IMPLEMENTED IN ORDER TO HELP ACHIEVE THE GOAL OF OUR YOUTH MINISTRY PHILOSOPHY.

DEVELOPING A SCOPE & SEQUENCE

SCOPE: THE CONTENT. THE "WHAT" OF YOUR CURRICULUM.

> **YOU MUST DETERMINE THE SPECIFIC INFORMATION PRECEPTS, PRINCIPLES, DOCTRINES, ETC. THAT ARE NECESSARY TO EFFECTIVELY REACH OUR GOAL.**

SEQUENCE: THE "WHEN" AND "HOW OFTEN" OF YOUR CURRICULUM.

TAKING THE SCOPE AND DECIDING WHEN SPECIFIC TOPICS ARE "AGE-APPROPRIATE" AND THE LEARNER IS "AGE-READY."

ALSO DECIDING HOW OFTEN REINFORCED.

Distractions in Teaching

1. Intrinsic
    - Family problems
    - Boy/girl friend issues
    - Accomplishments/miscues
    - Current events
    - Appetite (food/drinks)

2. Extrinsic
    - Room Temperature
    - Set-up of the room
    - Lighting
    - Seating (chairs/arrangement)
    - Presentation (master teaching/small group teaching)
    - Variety in methods (technology, media, drama's, role playing, sidebar participants)

YOUTH & MISSIONS

YOUTH & MISSIONS

I. Three basic goals of motivating youth toward world missions

   A. Goal #1-_____
   1. World Christians are day-to-day disciples for whom Christ's global cause has become the integrating overriding _____ for all that He is for them. Like disciples should, they actively _____ all that their Master's Great Commission means. Then they _____ on what they _____.

   2. Missiologist _____ defines a "world Christian" this way: "As a child of the kingdom the believer then becomes a world Christian. By calling he belongs to a universal fellowship-the Christian church. By conviction he proclaims a universal message-the Christian Gospel. By commitment he owes his allegiance to a universal king-Jesus Christ. By vocation, he is part of a universal movement-the Christian mission".[2]

   3. The youth leader's challenge is to produce young people who are thinking about a world _____ _____. To be a teenage "world Christian" is to be uncharacteristically unselfish with _____, _____, _____, and _____.

   B. Goal #2-_____
   1. Broaden their perspective so that they consider missionary service a _____ _____ of Christian obedience.

   2. Without the development of _____, young people will perpetuate _____.

   C. Goal #3-_____
      Teenagers must:
   1. Be helped to understand the church's _____ in missions throughout the world.

   2. Be helped to understand their _____ in world missions.

   3. Be helped to understand the _____ and _____ influences at work on foreign fields and against which the Gospel is struggling.

---

[2] "Youth & Missions, Expanding Your Students' World View," by Paul Borthwick. Victor Book, 1988, pg. 28.

FOUNDATIONS OF YOUTH MINISTRY

      4. Be given the chance to help solve the problems of _____, _____, and _____ that they might help those less fortunate to find opportunity to find life, fulfillment, and redemption in Christ.

II. The Example of Church Leaders and Pastors
    A. _____ _____ overseas to visit missionaries

    B. "_____" a missionary and their family

    C. Introduce church family to missions

    D. Develop _____/_____/_____ that would make it easier to go on mission opportunities

III. Exposure To New Cultures
    A. Building Cross-Cultural Appreciation
        1. _____
        2. _____
        3. _____!
        4. _____

    B. Cultural Sensitivity
        1. _____
        2. _____
        3. _____

    C. Staying Healthy
        1. Bring sunscreen, a hat, and keep your shoulders covered when you work. The sun in many of the places we are going is more severe than we are accustomed to. Severe sunburn can incapacitate you for days.

        2. In foreign countries, do not go hopping into fresh water without first asking your missionary hosts. In many areas of the world, bodies of fresh water contain parasites that enter through your skin. These parasites are very difficult to get rid of and could be fatal if unattended.

        3. Do not walk around with bare feet. Hookworm (another parasite) enters through bare skin. When digging with your hands, wear gloves, and when walking around, wear shoes, slippers, or flip-flops.

4. Be very cautious about green leafy vegetables. The general rule of thumb is this: if you cannot peel it, boil it; if you cannot boil it, don't eat it! Do not eat any fruit or vegetable raw unless you wash it and then peel it.

5. About water: Some statistics report that 80 percent of diseases in the Third World are transmitted through impure water. Ask local missionaries if the water is all right to drink. Remember, if the water is not healthful, you cannot swallow it in the shower, use it to brush your teeth, or have it in your drinks in the form of ice.

6. Expect that you will get diarrhea. Even slight changes in our own country can upset the intestinal tract. To control diarrhea, bring with you Kaopectate, Lomotil, or Parapectolin (the latter two require a prescription).

7. To prevent unnecessary trips to the clinic or hospital while your team is serving, bring Band-aids with you, get an updated tetanus shot before you go, and remember any needed allergy medicines.

8. Ask about other required shots. Yellow fever, cholera, gamma globulin, and typhoid are the most commonly required. Antimalarial treatment (usually chloroquine) may also be recommended.

9. Be careful with insects and animals. If you swim in salt water, be careful with spiny urchins or stinging jellyfish. On land, tarantulas, blackwidow spiders, scorpions, and "fire ants" are all potential dangers, not to mention snakes. In general, be careful; do not antagonize or attack them. Few are deadly, but many of these creatures can make you very ill. Treat them with respect!

10. While adventure, experimentation, and involvement is encouraged, do not to take unnecessary risks. You are most valuable and useful if you are healthy.

IV. Adventure in Missions
    A. Adventures in _____
    B. Adventures in _____
    C. Adventures in _____
    D. Adventures in _____

The Essentials of Planning a Mission Trip

Why a Mission Trip

Brings _____ to a group

Students come back with a new perspective

    The world does not revolve around them
    Can understand the ministry of _____ others
    God can use them for His glory
Aligns students with you and your leadership
Brings a renewed enthusiasm for the things of God

Location
Home missions
Foreign missions
    Overseas
    Bordering Countries

Pre-trip
Need to know who, what, when, where
Safety/Security
First Aid/Medical Personnel
Medical _____ plans
Where you are staying
    Hotels
    Homestays
    Tents
Who is going to feed you?
What are you going to eat?
    _____/_____ can make or break the spirit of a trip
    Water
Where do you "go"?
Where do you shower?
What you are going to do?
    Evangelism
    Ministry Teams
    Service/Work Projects
Who should go? (age/spiritual appropriateness)

Promotion
Must sell this idea to church leadership, parents, kids
Brochure

Keep in front of church/group
Videotape
Someone who's been there
Display

Timetable
A year in advance is preferred
Six months before
One month before
The week before
The day before

Forms, Forms, and more Forms
Release forms
Medical forms
Identification

Financing
Kids pay entire fee
Church pays all or a portion of costs
Youth group engages in fundraising
Great opportunity for kids to see how God can provide
Manage the money (some cash; mostly traveler's checks; dummy wallet; money belt; keep receipts)

Transportation
Getting there
Getting around when you're there

Evening Programs (when schedule permits)
A time to _____
A time to _____
A time to _____
A time to _____/_____
A time to let students know of the next days schedule
  (HINT: Give them one day at a time)

Rules
No _____
Be _____
Treat the opposite sex like a brother or sister
No drinking/illegal drugs
Be on _____
No _____ meetings
Always be in groups of _____ (preferable with at least one guy in group)

FOUNDATIONS OF YOUTH MINISTRY

Cultural Sensitivity
Phrases/words
Gestures
Clothing Styles
_____
_____

Laughing with, not at
Become a cultural _____ and _____
Don't publicly compare
Don't put down

Pre-Trip Orientation
Location and Date of Departure/Arrival
Phone #'s
Payment Schedule
Form Schedule
Q/A time
Video Clip
Brief challenge to establish a servanthood attitude, the need of those to be ministered to, and develop enthusiasm
Expectations/goals of the trip
What to Bring List
What Not to Bring List

Post-Trip
Need a time of _____
Need a time of rest and relaxation
Need a time of _____
Need a time of _____
Need a time of _____